Stock Trading for Beginners

The Complete Guide to Trading and Investing in the Stock Market

Table of Contents

Introduction

Congratulations on downloading *Stock Trading for Beginners* and thank you for doing so.

The following chapters will discuss the steps you need to know to get started on the stock market. Many people worry that investing in the stock market is not for them. They may have heard stories about how some people lost their savings by jumping into a stock and risking it all. The tips and strategies in this guidebook are going to prevent you from ending up being an investor like that.Instead, this guidebookwill show you how to exactly make money trading on the stock market.

Inside this guidebook, we are going to discuss everything you need to know to get started on investing in the stock market. We will start out with some basics about the stock market before moving on to how to tell the differences between some securities, how to choose a good stock, how to look over an SEC report, and even how to get the right trading platform for you to be successful.

We are also going to discuss some strategies that you can use to buy and sell the right stocks at the right time. We will look at some methods to figure the true value of a stock, as well as how to do a fundamental analysis and recognize some stock patterns. Moreover, we will discuss other strategies to make you successful. We will end this guidebook with a discussion on the best tips you can follow to help avoid a loss and gain a profit on the stock market.

There are plenty of books on this subject on the market, thanks again for choosing this one! Every effort was made to ensure it is full of useful information. Please enjoy!

Chapter 1: How to Enter the Stock Market

The stock market is a very exciting field to invest in. This is a very large industry where billions of dollars are traded each day.

There are thousands of different stocks that you can choose to trade. With its diversity, you can find a stock that interests you and works for your budget as long as you take some time to explore it. Anyone who has a little money can get into the stock market and earn an income.

While anyone can get into the stock market, it is important to be able to spend some time exploring and fully understanding it before jumping in. Those who have studied the market for some time are the ones who tend to do the best when it comes to investing.

What Is the Stock Market?

The stock market is going to refer to all parties involved in the selling and buying of shares, bonds, and other securities of a publicly listed company. An important part of the free economy, the stock markets have two segments, namely, the primary and the secondary markets.

The primary market is made up of early-stage companies, or those who are trying to sell shares in order to gain resources for themselves. They do this through an initial publicoffering or an IPO. Thanks to how the stock market works, companies are ableto acquire funds by selling their stock to public investors. In return, these investors gain partial ownership of the company.

For the most part, long-term trends show that the market as a whole is on an upward trajectory, and many investors are interested in adding stocks to their portfolio. Many people have made their fortunes with the stock market, butyou really haveto study it, be disciplined, and have some sound thinking behind any investment decision.

Making money from the stock market does not have to be difficult. Just like any other kind of investment, it is possible to master and be good at this with time, practice, and lots of studying. You can easily make a living on the stock market, but you need to be rational andthink through things because many people have also lost all their resources from just one bad investment. This is where the stock market gets its bad reputation.

Many investors who jump in without thinking find themselves greatly disappointed because they lost everything. If only they had started with a good strategy and invested only on what they could afford to lose, the stock market could have been their key to great success.

What Is the Difference Between Investing and Speculating?

To keep it simple, an investor is someone who decides that it is time to make their money work for them. They may use some of their own savings to purchase a stock and then earn any paid profits as long as they hold on to that stock.

Investing is going to have rules. Anyone can become an investor, but you can only get ahead in the market if you learn the right strategy and agree to stick with the rules.

When you do not act within the rules, you may become a speculator without even knowing. A speculator is someone who only pays attention to short gains. They will rush into a position and make themselves more vulnerable at the same time. Now, there is a difference between a speculator and a day trader. Day traders study the market, and they plan to be in it for a long time. They just make a lot of trades throughout the day, but they have a plan and they know what they are doing along the way.

A speculator is just someone who wants to jump in, make money overnight, and be done with it. This happened a lot with the rise of Bitcoin. Bitcoin started at $1 per coin in 2009. It steadily rose until it almost reached $20,000 a coin by December 2017. Many people jumped on to this, hoping to see another price increase and not looking at what this cryptocurrency is about. Almost overnight in early January 2018, the Bitcoin crashed down to $10,000. It now holds steady around $6,000 to $6,500 in worth.

An investor would have seen this as trouble. They would have known that they would lose money because the cryptocurrencywould not stay at that level with the way it was set up. Savvy investors would have stayed away and picked another option. A speculator, however, would have joined the Bitcoin market in December and lose all their money by January.

Do not be a speculator when you join the stock market. There are times when a stock will surprise you. This may allow you to make a lot of money, but you need to concentrate on how the market works and whether it is actually a smart investment for you.

Understanding More About the Stock Market

The stock market plays a big role in driving the economy. It is characterized by trading equities and some other securities from a publicly listed company. One popular investingstyle in the stock market is addingfunds to a public company in orderto gain partor full ownership. This means the investor is entitled to some of the profits from that company. A successful investor will receive more in dividends than the capital they originally gave out.

As we mentioned, there are two types of markets, which are the primary and secondary markets.

*Primary market.*This is where company shares are traded through an IPO. You can also view this as a direct trade between the investor and the company.

Secondary market. This is when investors trade among themselves, while the associated company for the security is excluded.

The two factors that help determine the price of a public company's stock are the volume of shares and the value of the company. In an IPO, the company needs to stash away any windfall. Once the stock grows enough in time to generate revenue, it will be the turnof the investor to profit from it. The company, on the other hand, will not profit.

The trading of stocks occursin an exchange. These exchanges play a role in facilitating trades between the buyers and the sellers. Most of the time, these are going to be done electronically. These exchanges are found in almost all capital cities in the world. In the United States, the two most known exchanges are the NASDAQ and the New York Stock Exchange. The U.S. Securities and

Exchange Commission, or the SEC, is an independent agency of the federal government thatoversees these exchanges and ensures fair play and investor protection.

Supply and demand drives the price of a stock. If there is a ton of buzz around a company, then, more investors will be interested in trading theshares of the company. Profitable companies can also see the same rise in their stock prices.

There are different types of shares that you can purchase, including, but not limited to the following:

- Ordinary shares
- B-ordinary shares
- Exchange traded funds
- Preference shares
- N-ordinary shares

There are also two types of securities that can be traded on the stock market, namely, listed and over-the-counter securities. The listed securities need to meet all the listing requirements of an exchange and must secure approval from the SEC. On the other hand, over-the-counter securities will be traded between peers and will be handled by dealers. These over-the-counter securities often do not appear on an exchange, which means they do not have to meet SEC requirements. There are times when they can prove to be a good investment, but they also involve more risk than normal securities.

Each type of stock you choose to work with will come with its own risk. You have to determine which method is going to be the best for your needs. You can choose a long-term investment in a company that is already doing well and is returning good dividends. Or, you can take a bit more risk and go with a new company that you predict will do so much better and give you huge returns in the future. As an investor, you have to know the difference between these two options. You must also have a system in place to determine how much risk you are willing to take on.

Should I Go with Stocks or Options?

Stock trading and options are the best choices when it comes to investing. Many brokerage firms will offer both these services to their investors, but how do you know which one is the best for you?

First, let us take a look at a stock. A stock is simply a fraction ofownership in a company that you can purchase. You can technically own as many shares of thecompany's stock as you can afford, as long as someone is willing to sell them to you.

An option is a little bit different. This is not really a form of ownership, but it is more of a right to own or trade a certain investment. You own the investment, but not a part of the company it belongs to. When you work with an option, you have the right to buy or sell a stock at a certain value within a specific period of time.

There are also no rules on how long you need to hold onto a stock. You can set a timeline on how you plan to make money, as well as the strategy that you want to go with. However, when you have an option, it will have an expiration date. This means you have until that expiration date to decide if you are going to use that option, or purchase that option. This gives you a specific time period to execute a purchase or a sale at a certain value. You can keep the option of running for as long as you would like. Some of these options last for an hour, while others evenlast for a few years. It all depends on which option you go with.

Stocks are a bit different. You can technically hold onto them until you die. But there are some who have a shorter timeline on holding these stocks. For example, a day trader may trade their stocks multiple times throughout the day. These investors are looking to capitalize on the little increases that occur in a stock on a daily basis. Then, there are long-term investments in the stock market where a trader will hold onto the stock for a long time, earning dividends on it each quarter.

The one you want to go with is going to depend on your level of experience in investing and how much risk you want to take on. Often, options are seen as riskier because you are betting on the price staying or moving to a specific level over time. This is the opposite for many stocks, which can stay pretty secure and can be done over the long term. Regardless of their differences, both can be great ways to earn an income and get your money to work for you!

Chapter 2: The Differences Between Stocks, Mutual Funds, Index Funds, and ETFs

When you enter into the stock market, you have several options to help you make a profit. Some people choose to work on their own and would just like to purchase individual stocks that suit their needs. Others may want to play it safe or increase their buying power by working with a mutual fund. And still, others find their trading strategy to bea bit different from either of these. Let us take a look at the differences between some of the investment choices you can make when you enter the stock market.

What Are Stocks

First, we need to look at stocks and what they are about. To keep things simple, a stock is a share in the ownership of a company. The investor who holds onto the stock has a claim on the assets and earnings of that company. The more stocks in a company you acquire, the more ownership you have in that company.

Now, this does not mean that you technically own the corporation.Owning thestock does give you some power though. When you own a stock, Itmeans you might have the right to vote on importantdecisions for the company. You can also receive dividends off the profits of a company. It also allows you to sell those shares of the company whenever you want to do so.

If you are able to own the majority of the shares in acompany, you will see that your voting power increases, allowing you to indirectly control the way the company goes.

As a majority owner, you may have more power to nominate and appoint the board of directors. In a publicly listed company, a shareholder gets to voteon who sits on the board. The number of your votes, however, is dependent on how many shares of the company you own.

This is important becausethe board
directs the goals and activities of the
company. The board is also involved in
the appointment ofpeople to top
management roles like the chief
executive officer, chief operating officer,
and the chief financial officer.

Your voting poweralso becomes very
apparent any time a company buys
another. The acquiring company does
not go around and buy the building,the
employees, and the chairs. Instead, it
goes and buys up all the shares. The
company usually needs the approval of
its shareholders for any proposed merger
or acquisition to push through.

When you are investing in the stock
market, being unable to manage the
whole company is probably not that big
of a deal. Most shareholders are
interested in receiving dividends off the
profits of the company. The more shares
you own, in this sense, the larger portion
of the profit you will get. There are times,
however, when the companywill not

payout dividends. Instead, the company will reinvestitsprofits back for its own growth. These are known as retained earnings, but it can still be a way to make money.

A company will issue stocks to raise capital, grow itsbusiness, and undertake new projects. There are some bigdifferences between an investor directly buying shares from the issuing company, or from an investor buying theshares from another shareholder. When a corporation issues its stocks, they are doing it to gain money to help their growth.

When you think about investing in the stock market, the first thing you probably think about is stocks. The day-to-day price fluctuations of these stocks can be varied, but if you stick with them for the long term, they usually tend to trend upwards. If you get a bad stock, you can end up losing money as it fails. But generally, the market and the value of the stocks will continue to grow. The company gets the funding they need to expand and grow, and you get a chance to earn a profit on the dividends if you invest wisely.

Mutual Funds

Another option you can go withis mutual funds. Mutual funds are perfect for any investor who wants to be able to reduce their risks rather than strike out alone. Mutual funds are high-flying projects where the resources of many people are pooled together in order to purchase scaled securities. The funds will be contributed by various investors in the group in exchange for a slice of ownership in the fund. The fund has a manager, who will take the time to study the market and eventually make the best decisions for everyone in the group. While the manager makes the decisions, it will be the board who will authorize it.

In most instances, these mutual funds need to have goals. The manager is then responsible for making sure that the fund reaches those goals.

The shares that are found in a mutual fund will be bought using the fund's present Net Asset Value, or NAV. This value is derived by dividing the securities value of the total shares. Having a stake in a mutual fund is often more secure and rewarding compared to purchasing shares from a bunch of random companies. They also work well because smaller investorsare able to own a portion of the value in the fund's portfolio.

Even if the investor is not able to invest a lot of money, they can join a mutual fund and increase their odds of making money. Considering most fund managers have a lot of experience in the stock market and are earning consistently high returns on the choices they make for investing, it is often safer and more profitable to use mutual funds rather than just trading on the stock market on your own.

To keep it simple, mutual funds are going to take money from many investors and pool it together. This helps give individual investors more buying power than they had on their own. The fund manager is able to choose which securities are the best for the whole company to invest in. They will work to make a profit for everyone involved in the mutual fund. The investor benefits because they get more buying power, they can earn a profit, and they automatically get diversity in their portfolio this way.

There are many types of mutual funds that you can try out. Some of the ones that you should consider are:

- Target date funds
- Smart beta funds
- Alternative funds
- Equity funds
- Sector funds
- Money market funds
- Balanced funds
- Index funds
- Fixed income
- Funds of funds

There are different reasons why you would like to purchase from a mutual fund rather than pickstocks on your own and buy them. Some of these reasons include:

- *Professional management.* Most investors do not have the information, skills, or time to invest on their own. With a mutual fund, a professional manager is going to take over and make investment decisions for you.
- *Diversification.* There is no other way to get as much diversification as quickly as possible thanwith a mutual fund.
- *Economies of scale.* A mutual fund is going to purchase and sell in big volumes, so they get reduced fees. They can also invest in bigger proportions compared to what a single person can do.
- *Simple.* Getting into a mutual fund only takes a few clicks to be done.
- *Lots of transparency.* Mutual funds need to meet certain

regulations so you know they are safe to invest in.

- *Ease of access*. You can easily purchase or sell your mutual fund holdings on the exchange at any time.
- *Custom*. You are able to search around and find a mutual fund that aligns with your goals and with what you want to invest in.

Index Funds and ETFs

An index is a collection of securities that will represent the value of an economic sector. Investors track indices to help determine how badly or well a market sector is doing. An index fund, on the other hand, is going to be a collection of securities investments that will involve tracking market performance. Investors are going to gain any time the market goes up. These index funds are a viable option because they can offer you a lot of exposure to the market with lower expenses, compared to other options such as hedge funds.

These index funds are sometimes known as a form of passive fund management, and they will bring in more gains compared to mutual funds. Most of these index funds are going to track the S&P 500, which is the top 500 public companies in terms of market capitalization in the NASDAQ or the New York Stock Exchange.

Before you decide to purchase one of these index funds, you need to understand what the index is and then check the rate in which your index fund will replicate the gains of its index. And while this is sometimes seen as a more passive form of investing, the portfolio manager needs to figure out how to track the index to make the most money.

Now, an exchange-traded fund or ETF is going to be a collection of securities investments whose shares can be purchased or sold on the stock market at a set market price. This is similar to what you would find in a mutual fund because it tries to pool resources from many investors before investing it in the most profitable markets. The ETF needs to have a goal for investing and a sense of direction.

Most of these ETFs are only going to invest in securities, and they must make sure that they operate using the guidelines set by the SEC. As an investor, there are several types of ETFs that you can choose to invest in, including the following:

- Active or passive management
- Fixed bonds or income
- Income and dividend
- Currency
- Commodities
- International
- Sector and industry
- Broad market
- Capitalization-weighted
- Factor-based strategies
- Hedged or leveraged strategies

These ETFs are going to be listed on an exchange and you can either purchase or sell shares during trading hours. The price of the ETF is going to be determined by market forces. You can buy these ETFs through a broker at any time during normal trading hours. These are great options because they are going to promote a lot of portfolio diversification, which can really reduce your risks and increase your potential profits. The operating fees that come with these types of investments are also quite a bit lower compared to hedge funds and mutual funds. ETFs are also associated withhigh liquidity, making it easier to sell them if you ever decide to get out of the market.

As you can see, there are a lot of options when it comes to choosing the right investmentfor your needs. You should carefully consider each one to figure out which will bring you the most profits with the least amount of risk. You should also factor in your own personal trading style when you begin working with the stock market.

Chapter 3: How to Choose the Right Stock When You are Ready to Invest?

Now that we know a little more about the stock market, it is time to learn more about which stock is the best for you. There are thousands and thousands of different stocks available for you to invest in, but not all of them are going to be right for your investment. The first thing you need to do is to learn which stock is going to help you actually earn a profit on your money. Some of the ways you can tell if a stock is a right investment for you include:

Choose Stocks in a Market You Understand

The first thing you need to do when you want to purchase a stock is to find a field that you know a little bit about. With the diversity of the market, this field could be banking, energy, health care, insurance, real estate, and tech, among others.

It is easier to invest when you know about the market the stock is in. You would then have a better understanding of what drives that market, the competition in that market, and how people in that market would react when something changes. You would want to do as much research on the market as possible, even if you already have a good understanding of how it works from the beginning.

Look at the National Market

The NASDAQ and the New York Stock Exchange make up the vast majority of trading volume not just in the United States, but also in the whole world. But this does not mean that you are limited to just working with the stocks on these exchanges. You can also choose to look at some of the other exchanges throughout the world. You may find that the Japan Stock Exchange, the London Stock Exchange, the Euronext, or the Shanghai

Stock Exchange have some better options for your investments.

Additionally, you may find that thecurrent state ofthe economy in one country may be quite a bit different in another country. For instance, Canada may have a bull market where stock prices are increasing, while India may have a bear market where stock prices are dropping. Each country is going to be different so it is often best for you to pick stocks based on an exchange that you are quite familiar with. For most people, looking at the U.S. market is the best option.

Do You Know Much About the Company?

You can't just pick a stock because it looks like it is doing well. You need to have as much information about the company as possible before you choose to invest. Investigate and see what you can come up with. Some of the things you need to look out for when deciding whether the company is a good investment or not include:

- What the company does to make profits
- Where is the company based out of
- The industry the company is in
- Thecompetitors of the company
- Updates on what the company is doing or is going to do in the future

This does not mean that you only have to invest in companies that you know a lot about, but it can help. If you choose to invest in a company that you are not really familiar with, then, you need to do enough research to fully understand what they are about before you purchase a stock. This information is going to be really critical when it comes to how much success you will find with this investment.

Look at the Trends for the Price

The next thing we need to look at is how the value of that stock is trending. While the market may move on an upward trend, each stock is going to have its own personal trendthat you need to follow. You want to watch and see whether the price is going up or down. If you see that the price is going down, and it has been trending this way for some time, then, it may be best to find another stock to invest your money in.

These price trends can be really helpful, but you also need to take a look at how long those trends are occurring and if there were any big changes that caused them to happen. There is always a chance that the stock will go back up if it starts to decline, but this is not always the case. You will need to figure out why the price trend is going down for that company and then figure out if it is likely to go back up.

Work with Some of the Moving Averages

One method that you can work with when investing is to watch the moving average of your stock. This is going to be the series of averages of a stock's price over a long period of time. To do this, we are going to look at an example of establishing a 14-day moving average. This is so we can get a good idea of how the stock is changing, without having to be bogged down by all the ups and downs of the company.

1. To start, take a look at the closing price of the stock. Grab that number from each of the past 14 days.
2. Add those 14 closing prices together.
3. Divide the number you got in the last step by 14.
4. This gives you the full moving average.
5. Go through and get as many of these moving averages for 14 days as possible. You can compare March 1 to 14, March 2 to 15, March 3 to 16, and so on to check if there is a big change or not.

When you use as many of these moving averages you get, it helps give you a better idea of how that stock changes. Day traders are going to benefit more if they do a shorter time frame for a moving average. You can also combine some long-term and short-term averages if you need a clearer picture of how the stock has been faring in the market. This is useful for all investors who want to get an idea of how individual stocks, as well as the market, are changing over time.

Check out the Company's Relationship with Their Revenue and Their Debt

A business that is able to bring in more revenue than debt is clearly doing well. It is going to have enough funds to manage all its operations, coverexpenses and debts, and pay its employees. Although the revenues of a business are important, you also have to look at the debts because if these are too large for the amount of revenue the company makes, it can spell disaster. The debts are going to include any expenses for loansto purchase new assets or to manage the salaries of the employees.

You can take a look at the gap that occurs between the debt and the revenue, and how it has changed throughout time. Financial documents from the company will reveal what was able to influence those totals and how they may change in the future.

Compare How That Stock Is Doing Compared to Other Choices You Can Make

The next thing you need to investigate is how other similar stocks are doing in the market. This gives you a yardstick to measure that stock and see if it performs in a similar or in a very different manner from other similar companies on the market. You will want to check out multiple stocks in the same field.

If you are trying to work with a retail stock, you need to check at least four retail-oriented stocks to see which is going to be the best for you. You can also take the time to look at the backgrounds of those companies to give you a better idea on how they are functional or profitable.

If you do this analysis and find that the stock is performing better than some of the others in the same industry, find out why. It may be that the company is doing something good that will keep the trend going. But it is also possible that this was just a small change in the market and the price would not be able to last. If you find that the stock is doing poorly compared to some of its competitors in the industry, it may be better to avoid that stock, or at least consider why it is not doing the best at that time.

Each investor is going to have their own criteria when it comes to picking out the perfect stock to start their investment on. But having a list of things to check out when it comes to looking at stocks can make things easier. It helps you avoid being distracted from focusing your attention on a stock that will do well over the long term, rather than over the short term.

Chapter 4: Looking Over an SEC Report

Before we get into the specifics of joining the stock market and some of the strategies you can use, we need to take a look at the SEC reports. This is a great way to learn more about the stocks that you want to invest in. Any company that is public and has stock will need to release one of these reports each year. You can look through the data in these reportsin order to find the best stocks to invest in. Let us take a look at these reports and explore what information you can find inside of it.

The Background of This Report

SEC reports are documents that all publicly traded companies need to submit to the SEC each year. These reports have been a requirement since 1933 when the Securities Act was passed following a big stock market crash a few years before. The U.S. government requires this as a way to ensure that allfinancial reports from these companies are specific and transparent before anyone tries to trade with them.

These reports are important to investors. They help investors make sensible decisions about the stocks and companies they want to invest in. This would help discourage investors from making a stock purchase that they do not really understand, something that was at the bottom of the big stock market crash of 1929.

By having a business share all its financial information with the public, the SEC is trying to ensure thatfraudulent activities would happen less often. Every business you want to invest in will need to have these kinds of reports available.

These reports need to be detailedto help prove how much the company is worth and how they run their business. If the business fails to provide enough information in these reports, it is highly suspicious and you may want to consider investing in another company.

The 10-K Report

The first report that you can look through is the 10-K. This is just a basic document that can give you a good overview of theannual performance of a company. It will contain a lot of the information on the company, except for the electoral processes which the investor does not need to know about.

This is a vital document because it gives you a good understanding of how the business works. It helps you see how the company is running and what are its different holdings. The information you get from here can be very valuable. If you just want the basics to help compare a few companies before diving in, then, this is the report that you need to look through.

Summary of Operations

The first point you can look through in your 10-K report is the summary of operations. This is going to include a lot

of different information about the
company including:

- *The background of the business.*
  This will provide you with
  information on what the company
  does or what it sells.
- *The business strategy.* This could
  include information on how the
  business is working to move
  forward.
- *Information on current offerings.*
  This must include information on
  both the non-physical and physical
  items that the company has. It can
  also show any service that the
  company is providing outside of its
  products.
- *Competition points.* This section is
  not going to specifically name a
  competitor, but it will include
  information on how other parties
  in that field would offer certain
  services or products. This is a good
  place for the company to show
  itself as competitive and different
  from others on the market.

- *Research and development data.*
  This section should include any
  information on what the business
  is doing to find new products and
  make them available. It also has
  information on the amount of
  money the company spends to do
  this.
- *Trademarks, copyrights, patents,
  and licenses.* If there are any new
  applications for these things, they
  need to be included. This helps the
  investor to know if the company is
  committed, and if they are
  prepared in case a legal issue
  comes up. You may find that it is
  beneficial to invest in a company
  that cares about its efforts. There
  would not be a ton of information
  here though.
- *Foreign information.* This section
  means any operations that the
  company has outside of its base
  country.
- *Business seasonality.* This is going
  to show you when the company
  does a lot of its business. Some

companies have more seasonal demand than others.

You can take the information on this report in order to come up with the right strategy for investing. It may tell you the best time to invest in the market, whether or not a company is doing well, or any other information you need to make informed decisions.

The Financial Outlook Information

The next thing you can look through is the financial outlook information. This is going to show any of the financial approaches that the company is currently using. The information that may be present in this part of the report will include the following:

- The net revenue the business earns from its operations
- The gross margin
- The operating income
- The costs the company spends on research and development

- The effective tax rate
- The total value of any assets the business has
- The debt the business holds
- How many employees the business has

This financial information is going to include some historic points for you to look at as well. You can see whether the business is doing better or worse because there are certain prior points to compare. An annual report usually compares its performance for the current year with the past year. This gives you important insight into the business and whether it is going to last.

The Balance Sheet

Next on the list is the balance sheet. This is going to show a lot more financial information for the shareholder. It can give them a good look into whether the company has enough revenue to handle their debts and whether or not the investor will actually be able to make anything with that company. Some of the information that needs to be included on the balance sheet include:

- *The assets the company has.* This can include both long-term and short-term assets. They include things like property, equipment, investments, accounts receivable, inventory, and cash.
- *The liabilities of the business.* This could include any debts for long loans or bonds payable, customer advances, taxes or interests, and accounts payable for the company.
- *The equity of the shareholder's.* This is going to refer to the assets minus the liabilities. It is a measure of how healthy the company is. The total focus is on what the shareholders might be able to get back if the company is liquidated and the debts are paid off.

Income Statement

The income statement is another document you can read through when you are coming up with an investment strategy. This statement is going to show all the information on what the business is earning over time. This statement will have information on at least the last three years of the business. If you can get more information, that is even better because it provides you with a great picture of where the business is going and what has happened in the past few years.

10-Q Report

The 10-Q report is going to be similarin content with the 10-K report. However, it willfocus moreon the quarterly results of a business. It can include information about the financial statements for the business like different expenses, taxes, operating income, and gross profits. It can also include details about any big developments that occurred in the past quarter, ongoing legal proceedings, and risk factors, and some contracts that were set up with various groups during that time. This report can be useful to look at to determine how the company is doing right now.

A delay in submitting the 10-Q or the 10-K reports could also result in noncompliance with the listing standards of the New York Stock Exchange and the NASDAQ. If a company fails to gain compliance within the allowed period, its shares could be subject to delisting.

8-K Report

The 8-K report often goes by the name of Current Report. This is a statement that the company will issue whenever they have some major event that they must tell the public about now. Sometimes this report is just going to talk about something that caused the company to grow. But sometimes it will also talk about problems that are more difficult and can be red flags when it comes to your investment. This kind of report is filed so the company can discuss any of the following:

- Bankruptcy filing
- An introduction tosome key developments and issues that the shareholders need to vote on
- Any amendments to the Code of Ethics of the company
- Cases where the estimates that a business is expected to earn are dramatically altered in value. This usually happens if the value decreases.

- Any events that will make one of the company's financial obligations change
- The completion of a new and major acquisition plan
- When the company either enters or leaves a material definitive agreement
- The departure or appointment of certain company officers and directors

There are technically no limits on how many of these reports aresent out by a business. You would need to look at how the company lists them. Any company that uses these should be thorough and transparent when they publish these reports so that the investor knows what is causing the changes.

Schedule 13D

The Schedule 13D is another type of SEC filing that will cover details about who owns the shares of the company. A company needs to file this within 10 days after someone acquires five percent or more of any security. This helps other investors know how one person may be managing a lot of the shares of the company. It sometimes shows that one person is going to heavily influence that company. Some of the information that needs to be on the Schedule 13D include:

- Details on that security
- Information on the person who acquired that security. This can include the person's contact information and their background.
- The source of the funds for that transaction
- The reason that someone is acquiring these shares
- Any relationships or contracts that this investor has with others who are inside the business

- Letters and other documents that will show how the transaction occurred

This is an important document for an investor to look over because it gives a good idea on who owns the shares. If one individual or group starts taking over too much of the shares of a company, it could mean that some major changes are going to occur in the near future. You have to weigh whether this is a good thing or a bad thing before you decide to invest.

Form 144

The last form we are going to look at is the Form 144. This is going to cover how the stocks were made available to the public. This needs to be filed any time someone who is associated with the company plans to sell their stocks. This could be an important figure, such as the executive or director. This form is a simple document that is just two pages long. It needs to include the following details before being filed:

- The name of the company that issued the stock
- The title of the class of stock or security being sold
- The number of shares that are being sold at that time
- The names of any security exchanges that are being used
- How many of these shares are outstanding
- The market value of these shares
- Information on any of the other securities that the individual is selling, including any other shares that might have been sold in the past three months through them

The Form 144 needs to factor into your strategy when you look at how these shares are being made available to the public. Sometimes this kind of report is just showing that someone who works in the business is ready to retire so they sell off their shares. This usually is not a big deal and you can still get into the investment.

However, there are times when this is a sign that something big is going to happen in the business, such as someone else buying out a party of that entity. Depending on which party is involved and how that may change the business, this is definitely something that you need to watch out for and plan for before purchasing the security.

Chapter 5: How to Get into the Stock Market and PickOut the Best Trading Platforms

No matter what kind of strategy you decide to work with, it is going to be worthless if you are also not working with the proper trading platform. This trading platform is basically the program you are going to work with in order to make your trades directly. You can usually get one of these from a banking institution or your personal broker.

The trading platform is a necessity if you are an everyday trader. It allows you to do your trades from your own home electronically, so you do not have to go down in person to get the work done. The earliest of these platforms would let you find updated information on the stock prices, while allowing you to send signals about when you want to trade. The high-speed online world has changed so much that platforms can handle these transactions immediately and you can see real-time prices. All that

is needed to make this happen is an
online connection.

Analytics Points

A trading platform that you choose
should have various analytics that are
going to make it easier for you to identify
what stocks you want to work with.
While you should automatically be able
to find real-time charts and quotes about
any stock you want with this program,
you need to be aware of other things as
well. Some of these include:

News Feeds Are Important

Your chosen platform needs to have
some news feeds. These are going to
include some reports from news
organizations like Reuters and the
Associated Press. This news feed is going
to give you all the information that you
need on everything that happens in the
market. A platform can even search
through the feed if you need to find a

specific information on a stock. To look through the news feed, you just need the following steps:

- Look for the name of the stock you want to invest in.
- Check to see which exchange that stock is in and what symbol it uses
- Enter the content by listing it as the following: Abbreviation of exchange:symbol. This lets the program know what you are looking for.
- Check the results. These results might include details on the forecasts and even some SEC reports. Any outstanding events that need to be included will be here too.

The Right Security

You are going to be handling a lot of money through the platform. You will submit payments into the platform so you can purchase the stocks you want. And then, when you earn any profits, that money is going to come back to you as well. Depending on how much you trade, it is possible that you are going to have a lot of financial transactions.

With all of this money going back and forth, you want to make sure that your financial information is as secure as possible. If a platform has had trouble with a data breach recently, it may be best to go with someone else. Check if they have a good customer support system as well to ensure that someone will be there to help you if you have concerns with the security of your account.

Financial Points

Depending on the type of platform you choose, each one is going to have some additional financial fees that are specified by that trading platform. You need to know these fees because they are going to influence how much you will actually earn on each trade. Some of the things that you should focus on when it comes to picking out a trading platform include:

- Each platform is going to have their own fee structure for how much you will pay to do a trade. Some have a flat fee for a single trade or they may have a fee that is based on the number of shares you will purchase or sell. Sometimes the fees will end up cheaper if you do a bulk transaction.
- Options traders are going to have to pay extra for their contracts. The extra charge for each contract might not be much depending on the type of contract it is.
- An account minimum may be required in some cases. A lender may want you to keep a certain amount of money in the account before you decide to start trading. This helps them see that you are actually committed on trading on their platform. The amount is going to vary on each platform.
- Sometimes a platform will offer a special promotion. This could be a

cash bonus for any qualifying deposit. You might get $100 in extra money for trading if you put in $1000 or more into the account to start.

- Each platform has their own margin rates. The margin rates offered for options might be within a few percentage points of the current stock value.

What Are Some of the Best Platforms to Trade On?

The platform that you will use is going to vary depending on what kind of trading you would like to do, how much it costs, and which one seems to be the best fit for you. There are a lot of great options, but here are some of the best:

- Ally Invest
- TD Ameritrade
- TradeStation
- Interactive Brokers
- Charles Schwab

- EOption

If you are uncertain about which of these platforms is the best one for you, consider trying a few out. You can sometimes get a sample trade so that you can mess around on the platform and find which one is the most comfortable for your needs. If you find the one that feels more natural or is easier to use than others, then go ahead and give that a try!

Chapter 6: Understanding the True Value of a Stock

As you are looking through stocks and trying to figure out which ones you want to invest in, you are also going to learn which strategy is the best for you. But sometimes it is better to think about the underlying factors of a stock. The value of the stock may not be as good as the official total says, or the stock is overvalued. Pickingone of these stocks could result in you losing money when the market figures things out and the price goes down.

At the same time, a company may be doing well, but you may see thatthe stock price does not reflect this. This would be a good option to go with because the value is likely to go up as the market adjusts to reflect the total value of the company. You are going to need to look at several points to see how a stock is performing and if it is a good idea to go with that. Some points that you can look at include:

P/E Ratio

A good strategy to help you review the worth of the stock is knowing the price to earnings ratio, or the P/E ratio. This measurement is going to show you what investors are actually willing to spend on any given stock.

When you get a higher total here, it means investors expect to earn more over time from that option. When the total comes in low, this means the stock is undervalued. This could mean that this stock is an intriguing choice to go with. If you want to get this ratio, you need to do the following:

1. Take the current price of the stock.
2. Divide that number by the earnings per share, or EPS. If you do not have this number, the EPS is the net income divided by the outstanding shares.
3. This will give you the P/E ratio.

The total value that you get for the P/E ratio refers tohow much value the market is currently placing on the stock. When the ratio is higher, the stock market is going to value it more. When the market values it more, it means this is a stock that people want to purchase.

Let us look at an example of how this works. Looking at a stock, you may see that it has a market price of $26.26. Meanwhile, it has an EPS of $2.28. This is based on a net income of $697 million divided by 304.57 million outstanding shares of the company.

When you divide the value of the stock by the EPS, you are going to end up with a total of $11.52. This means that the average investor is willing to pay $11.52 for every dollar that the company earns. This is a cheap total because it shows that not too many investors are willing to go with this stock. If the P/E ratio is low, it shows that the stock is worth investing in if you want to find something less expensive on the market.

If you look at the company and see that they are losing money, there is going to be an N/A where the P/E ratio should be. You can technically go through and calculate a negative ratio and show that this company is losing money. It is often easier to use N/A to show that investors are not going to gain much when they invest in the company, because the company is not earning much and cannot put a number there.

Some investors still choose to go with this kind of stock because they can get it for a lower price. It all depends on the reason why the company is losing money. If they are losing because they went through an expansion, then, the number will go up in the near future, and it may be a good idea to invest while the stock is cheaper.

Now, what is the optimal P/E ratio that you want to trade on? It is hard to know whether a stock has a good P/E ratio. Each industry is going to be different. In the technology sector, a P/E ratio of 25 is a good option, but in some other industry,a ratio of 14 can be better. You need to experiment and see what looks the most enticing for you.

A Note AboutInflation

Before we move on, it is important to talk about inflation a bit when you are doing the P/E ratio. This measurement is often going to be a bit lower whenever the rate of inflation is high. This is because the earnings of the business are going to be skewed as inflation rises. It usually takes more than a few months for this inflation rate to make a big difference, but you do want to consider this in your calculations.

Price/Earnings Growth Ratio

The next type of measurement that you should look into when reviewing the true value of a stock is the price/earnings growth, or PEG, ratio. This is important because it is going to provide you with a measure of whether a particular stock is underpriced or if it is undervalued or not. It may also let you know if you are getting a huge bargain when you purchase a stock. You can measure the PEG ratio through the following steps:

1. Calculate the P/E ratio of the stock using the method we talked about before.
2. Divide this number by the annual EPS growth.

Let us look at an example of this. Say a business has a share price of $50 and an EPS of $4. The total may have gone up to $6 this year. Therefore, we are going to calculate the P/E ratio by diving 50 by 6, which gives us the answer of 8.33. Now, divide those earnings by taking 6 and dividing it by 5 while subtracting 1. This gives you an answer of 0.5 or 50 percent. The EPS growth is going to give you 50 percent. Divide the 8.33 by 50 and you get a PEG of 0.166.

The PEG might sound minimal, but this means that the stock is trading on a big discount compared to how much it is growing. This means that you could purchase the stock for way less than it is worth and as the company grows, you will make more and more. Over time, the value may help you get a great deal because the company is stable.

The point of doing the PEG is to give you a good idea of what you can expect from a stock that you might hold onto for some time. It shows that there is an upward trend in that stock. If you have a stock that has a favorable PEG, you might be more willing to hold onto it for longer because it is a great deal and will keep growing in the future.

The Price/Sales Ratio

The next strategy that you can choose to work with is the price/sales ratio or the PSR. Thereason you may want to use this one is because it compares the value the company's stock to its revenue. The stock of a company that has a good amount of revenue shows that the business is active and that is likely to stay around for some time. The steps that you can take toanalyze the PSR are:

1. Find the total number of the available outstanding shares.
2. Add the sales totals for each of the past 12 months.
3. Divide those sales totals by the number of shares.
4. Divide the current value of the share by the numbers you got in the third step.
5. This gives you the PSR based on how the past year of trading has gone for the business.

You can also change this up and replace the sales totals for the past 12 months with sales for the ongoing fiscal year if you want. This will give you an answer that is more relevant, but it will still probably be similar. Numbers for the current fiscal year can be used to help with this forecast. The measurement from the past 12 months is going to be more analytical,allowing you to see what has changed over time with the business.

If you see that the PSR is low, this means you can purchase the stock at a good discount. This shows how the company has a low cost compared to the revenues it is earning. If you want to purchase a stock, now is the perfect time to do it. This one is a good indicator because it is based on the sales of the company.

The business is going to have a hard time altering its sales totals compared to any estimates that the accounting team may try to showcase. The sales totals are going to be more stable and will work through cycles that change throughout the year. You can sometimes make a prediction about it, but you will not be able to fake it or make major changes to it like some otherestimations you can do for a business.

Analyze the Book Value of the Company

When you are trying to figure out the true value of a stock, you may want to spend some time looking at its book value. This is going to refer to the value of the assets that are in the stock, minus any liabilities and other intangible assets that the company is holding on to.

Simply put, the book value is going to refer to the value that an asset holds on the company's balance sheet. It will measure out what the shareholder will receive if the company has to liquidate tomorrow. This is going to be an estimate and you probably should not base all of your trades on it.The book value is something that you can explore though. The most important point aboutthe book value is that it is going to measure how a business will function. A business that has a better book value should not be one that has enough assets to keep it operational.

There are some issues that come with using this strategy because the book value may not be the best option every time. A business that is growing very quickly may not have an accurate book value because it is trying to accumulate more assets and wants to make some changes in the way it operates. Businesses that do not have a lot of physical assets also may not score high on this strategy.

In some cases, theintangible assets of a company could be a big problem. The reputation of a business may go through some damage or there could be a controversy or legal issue against one of the products or services that it offers. This would be hard to showin the book value of the company. Some of these, such as the reputation of the company, can be repaired over time, but for the shortterm, they could put some dents in how well a stock does.

The book value works the best if it is helping you when you are not sure whether a stock is the right one for you. Sometimes it can show you more information than the others. But this one does run into some issues that the others do not, and it is best to be careful about relying on this one on its own.

To make sure you are picking out a stock that is a good one and is offered at a deal, you may want to utilize a few of these strategies at once. This helps you see if the stock is really a good one to go with or not. If the company is strong on several of these strategies, then, it may be a good one to invest your money in. If it has mixed reviews between the strategies, you may want to reconsider using it or not. But if it fails on more than one, it is a good sign that you should stay away and not use it at all.

Chapter 7: How to Make Money in the Stock Market Using a Fundamental Analysis

A fundamental analysis is one of the first strategies that you can consider using. It is the study of the financial data of a company. The aim with this one is to determine the financial health and performance of a particular company. You are also trying to use this information to project whether the company is going to be weak or strong in the future. The fundamental analysis is a critical exercise because it helps investors decide whether the company is a good idea to invest in over the long term.

You should use this kind of analysis, at least in part, in any valuation you do on a security. Most investors tend to forget to use this one, but it can really help you find out if a security is as strong as it looks. You will look through several key metrics including projected future growth, interest rates, profit margins, and income to determine if this is the right choice for you.

Fundamental analysis is basically looking at the company and figuring out how the company is doing regardless of the price of the stock. Do they make good profits? Do they have a good plan for the future? Is their reputation good? Are they working on something that will really benefit them in the future? If these are all true and yet the stock is still lower than market rates, it may show that this is a good investment to get in to.

It is important that you have a few tools to help you do a fundamental analysis so that you can look past the face value. Some of the factors that you are going to use for this analysis include:

- *Earnings per share*. What percentage of the profits goes to the shareholders?
- *Price to earnings ratio*. What is the current share price to its EPS?
- *Dividend Yield*. What are the yearly dividends that are paid out

compared to the prices of the stock?

- *Dividend payout ratio.* What is the amount of dividends paid to the shareholders compared to how much the company makes?
- *Price to book ratio.* What is the book value of the stock when compared to its market value?
- *Price to sales ratio.* What is the share price compared to the revenue of the corporation?
- *Projected earnings growth*: By what percentage is the stock going to grow within a year?
- *Return on equity.* What is the company's return on equity? You can find out by dividing the net income of the company by the stockholder's equity.

The fundamental analysis can often be a great way to figure out if the company is offering shares at a discount compared to their worth. There are plenty of great stocks out there offering great dividends and good returns on investment, but other stockholders may undervalue them or may not even know them at all. You can use a fundamental analysis to help you find these stocks and get the most out of them.

Chapter 8: How to Recognize Patterns in a Stock

Some of the most popular strategies that you are going to use in the stock market will focus on patterns. These are cases where something is likely to change with a stock within a given time. Patterns can show how the stock price is moving, while still giving you a signal that something else will likely happen. There are a lot of different patterns you can work with.It is sometimes easy to figure them out once you learn how the stock is evolving. You can use these patterns to your advantage by having them help you plan your strategies for when to enter and exit a trade, or when figuring out the kinds of trades you should make. Let us take a look at a few of these and see what needs to happen so we can recognize some of the patterns.

Continuation or Reversal?

The most important thing you need to notice about these patterns is that there are two forms, and they often mean very different things when it comes to reading them.

- *Reversal.* This is when a current trend is starting to end. So, the stock may have spent some time going up, but with a reversal, it is going to start going down.
- *Continuation.* This shows that the price changes in the stock are going to continue along, even when the pattern is finished. The pattern may be a brief occurrence, but then, the stock is going to continue on unabated when that is done.

These points can be used to helpdetermine how you should trade a stock. You might consider purchasing a stock to sell later, or you could put in a call or put option depending on how you see that stock moving now and in the future. Either way, you can always invest in a stock, no matter whether it moves up or down in value.

One thing that you will notice with continuations and reversals is that they tend to go on for a long time. It is difficult for an investor to look at a trend and know how long it will last, but it is likely that the current trend will keep going on for some time.

Pennant

The pennant is a good pattern to look out for when trying to pick out a stock. This is going to be one of the continuation patterns that show how a stock can keep growing in value. At this point, the stock is going to appear to be struggling, trying to move up or down. But then, after some time, the stock is going to break out of the pennant and will keep moving toward the same position it had at the start. Some of the things this pennant can reveal to an investor include:

1. The value of your stock is either going to start decreasing or increasing sharply. The change may be the stock losing or gaining

a few percentage points of value. The change should be noticeable, no matter how valuable it is.

2. The value should then start to go in the opposite direction. So, it is going to slowly decrease after a sizeable increase, or it may go the other way around as well.

3. After some time, the values of the drops or the rises in the stock will start to minimize a bit. The stock might end up changing by just a few pennies in value after each candlestick. Sometimes the total volume or the range in which the stock changes value may be minimal.

4. Next, you are going to notice that the stock has little, and sometimes no change in value.

5. The pennant is going to end whenever the stock suddenly breaks out and sees a bit increase or decrease in its value. This should be a full continuation of what the stock experienced earlier in the game.

The layout of the pennant is going to let you know that the value of that stock is either stabilizing or it is about to break out. When the trading volume and the change in value shrink to almost nothing, it is a sign that something is going to happen soon. Sometimes, you will see that the value of that stock will go either up or down, depending on how the pennant started.

You will want to enter into this pennant when you notice that the changes that occur in each wave going down are very low totals. You can then watch to see how the pennant ends up being formed and check to see how the stock will break out. Then, place a stop-loss order on the opposite end of the trend to help provide a safeguard in case things do not go the way you want.

Bearish or Bullish?

A pennant has the power to be either bearish or bullish in value. When the pennant is a bullish one, it starts with a bit of a rally. The stock price is going to go up in the beginning, and then, it stabilizes. When the pennant has time to form, the stock is then going to move back up in value.

A bearish pennant is going to feature a price that will drop quite a bit before the pennant forms. The price may look like it is going up for a bit, and then,it will see a decline in value when the pennant ends.

Strategies to Help You Use a Pennant

There are a fewstrategiesthat can be useful when you are relying on a pennant. These include the following:

Watch for how changes in your candlestick patterns are going to vary when the pennant starts moving forward. Sometimes a majority of sticks in the pennant will end up going upwards or downwards. Either way, you might want to get into the trade after you see the pennant has formed all the way. You can also try to make some micro-transactions that last for a few minutes depending on where that pennant is flowing.It can be difficult though to determine how long the waves will move along and how many of the down or up candlesticks will be formed at this time.

Next, you can consider looking for as many of these pennants in a stock as possible. If you see many pennants there, it gives you a good idea on the sentiment around that stock. You may see that a bullish pennant is becoming bigger in size. This also shows that investors are liking that stock and are willing to invest in it.

Trade during the upside parts of the stock if possible. When you trade during this part, it helps you to identify some points where the value of the stock will probably increase in a short amount of time. This is going to work just for a brief time before something starts to shrink in value.

See if there are any big outliers to the pennant. This could be something like one stick in the middle of the pennant that is longer or larger than any others. This outlier often shows that there is some uncertainty in the stock. When you see the outlier starts to move down, this shows that the potential for an increaseis not as strong as it should be.

And finally, you should look at how long this pennant might be moving. Sometimes the pennant is strong to last for a few weeks or more, but usually, this just lasts for a few hours. This is because many people watch the stock market and they are going to respond pretty quickly to any changes that come in the stock. They may notice that a stock is trending up and is stable, so they may acquire it before the value bursts up again.

The Wedge Pattern

The next pattern you can watch out for is the wedge. This one is going tohave some similarities with the pennant, but with a different kind of shape. The wedge will be a pattern when the price wave is going to reverse. The range in the price of the stock is going to narrow after some time and then the stock will break out and either move down or up after the wedge is done.

So, how is the wedge different than the pennant? A wedge is organized based on the differences between stock prices that are in a specific range. There are three main types of wedges that you can watch out for.

- *Rising Wedge.* This is when the lows and the highs of this pattern keep on moving up. You can tell when this wedge is rising that the stock price is going to start a new downward trend. You need to sell your stock when the low on a rising wedge breaks beyond the lower bar because the stock is going to experience an even bigger decline soon.
- *Falling wedge.* The falling wedge is going to be the opposite of what we saw with the rising wedge. This is when the lows and the highs for the stock continue to decrease. You will want to purchase the stock

when it breaks out from the top part of your wedge.

- *Symmetrical wedge*. This kind of wedge is designed in a way that is very similar to a pennant. So if you have used a pennant, this one should look familiar. However, you will see that the narrowing of your gap is not going to be as close as you see with a pennant. You will be able to check and see if the wedge is going up or down by looking where it began on the chart.

The Cup and Handle Pattern

A cup and handle price pattern is going to look just like a cup in the shape of a "U" with a handle that goes slightly down. The right hand of the pattern is going to show a low trading volume and can be as short as just seven weeks or as long as up to 65 weeks.

A stock that is showing this kind of pattern is working to test out old highs. It is going to put selling pressure for any investor who purchased at those levels.This selling pressure is going to make price consolidation a tendency toward a downward trend for four days to four weeks. When that is done, it is going to advance even higher.This is considered a bullish pattern and it can help you figure out the best times to get into the market and make money.

When looking at your chart pattern, you want to make sure you go with a cup that has more of a "U"-shaped bottom than one that is sharper and looks like a"V."The cup and the handle should not be too deep as well. The volume should decrease as the stock price declines, and it should remain lower than the average you see in the base of the bowl. This helps you see the right time to make a purchase of the stock because you will able to make the most money.

To trade in this kind of pattern, you can place a stop buy order that is just a little bit about the upper trend line you see with the handle. Order execution is then only going to happen if you see this stock break that pattern. Traders may experience some excess slippage with this pattern and if you do an aggressive entry, you may enter a false breakout.

In addition, you can wait and see if the price closes above the upper trend of the handle and then, put a limit order above that breakout level. You can then attempt to get an execution if the price does retrace. This one is not always the best because you risk missing out on a trade if your pattern keeps on advancing and it does not pull back the way you want.

Head and Shoulders Pattern

You can also work with the head and shoulders pattern. This is a chart formation that is going to look like a baseline that has three peaks. Your two outer ones will be very similar in height and the middle one is going to be the highest. Theseare going to form when the price of the stock starts to rise. There are three main parts that come with the head and shoulders pattern:

- After a bullish trend is done, the price is going to rise to a peak before declining to form a new trough.
- The price is going to rise again in order to make a big peak. This one is going to be larger than the first one, sometimes by quite a bit.Then, it will decline again.
- The price is going to rise again, but this one will not go above like what you saw in the first peak and then, it will decline a little more.

This is often seen as a tug of war between investors and buyers. Whether the price of that stock ends up going down or up, it is going to be the result of how many investors or how many buyers there are. Those who believe that the price of that stock will go up are the bulls and those who think it will go down are the bears. If more of the shareholders are bears, then, the price will go down. But if more are bullish, then, the price is going to go up.

Triangles

Another pattern that you can explore is a triangle. This is going to be a continuation pattern, though there are times that it can end up turning into a reversal pattern. The triangle develops when the price changes in the stock are going to narrow. These steps show you exactly how this triangle pattern can get started:

1. A triangle is going to begin right when the stock heads up or down in value over a few trading periods.
2. The stock will start to go back to the opposite direction. This is going to form the line that is responsible for the other part of your triangle.
3. Your stock is going to move back and forth. The differences between these points will be smaller when the stock starts to move.

4. Eventually, the triangle is going to be formed. You will then need to be on a lookout for a breakout, which is when the stock will keep moving in the same direction that it did when the triangle started.

This is a good way for you to figure out when you should get into a trade. If you notice that a triangle is ready to start, you should watch and see which direction the trend is going. In most cases, the trend, after the triangle is done, will continue in the same direction as it started. Once the lines start forming, get in on the lower part of the triangle to get a better price for the stock and watch as the price starts to go back up. If you get in at a good time, you will be able to make a good profit on the work.

Chapter 9: When Should I Purchase Long and Sell Short?

One thing that you are going to hear a lot when you get into the stock market is to buy long or sell short. But as a beginner, these terms may be a little bit hard to understand. This chapter is going to explore these topics and what they can mean to your trading strategy.

You should buy long at any time you feel that the stock will grow more in value. It is going take more time to get a profit from your trades if you opt to buy and sell stock in the same day, but the potential for real gains are going to be greater with this method.

Then, you would want to sell short when you notice your market is falling. You want to try to sell the shares at a higher price, and then, purchase them back again at a lower price. This is different from when the long-trade requires you to actually acquire and hold on to the shares. We will explain these a bit more as this chapter goes on.

Trading in the stock market can take some time to get used to. You want to make sure you are always pickingthe right stocks and that you get in and out at the best times to make a profit. This chapter is going to show you some of the tips that you need to make this happen.

If you are looking at conventional wisdom, it suggestsfor you to buy long any time you see the stock price moving up, and then, sell short when you see the stock moving down. But there are often more variables at play when you actually get into the stock market, and we are going to take a look at how some of these will affect your decisions.

Investing with a Long Trade

First, we are going to take a look at a long trade. This is when you keep the trade for a period of time, which is something that you would not do if you want to be a day trader. Sometimes a long trade will be necessary to make money because there is a high potential for the value of the stock to go up. You need to watch for how the stock rises in value and how it moves in an upward line over time. More importantly, you have to look at what the future may hold for that stock.

You should stick with your long trade any time you want to limit your losses from trading right then and there. You can also use it if you are not interested in getting yourself into a margin deal. Working with a straightforward trade is often the best because it allows you to work with your own funds. Leveraging and other options can add to your profits, but they do put you at a risk of losing a lot of money as well.

Sometimes a stock is going to become more valuable over time because the company is strong. Trading long can be key to a big profit if you pick the right company. This can happen because the business is strong enough that its demand is going to last for a long time, or because it can consistently grow.

For example, Netflix is a good choice to go with for a long trade. Most people see Netflix as a way to stream or rent movies, series, and other original programming. Netflix started tradingon the NASDAQ at the beginning 2017 with its stock worth $130. By the end of2017, the stock rose to $200 as the company expanded its portfolio.

The key to finding a good company is to see the stock progressively growing. It can take some time, but you will make a lot of profits over time. You can also check how the business is able to sustain its growth. No matter what industry you are in, there are always going to be some new threats that can make it very hard for an investment to stay afloat. You need to make sure your chosen company is able to handle this.

Investing in a Short Trade

Another move that you can go with is a short trade. This is when you are going to sell shares that you borrow at a given time, and then, buy them back at any time that the market falls, all while making a profit. To do a short trade, you are going to have to pay a commission. If you borrowed shares at $50 each and then sell them at $80, you can make a profit of $30. However, you have to pay some commission on that profit. It is also possible that after you borrow the stocks, their value will go down and you will not make any profit from it.

A short trade is best when you have done enough research on the stock to know how it behaves. You need to look at how the stock has changed and how long you plan to borrow those stocks. You also need to know that sometimes the short sale will last for a few hours or a few weeks depending on your position.

Some investors wrongly assume that selling short is like doing a put option. But a short sale is going to include the actual sales of a business. You could end up losing a lot more money with this option if you are unable to match with the market the right way. A put option has the added benefit of being able to end the contract before your chosen date. Selling short, however, does not allow this. It becomes way riskier to go with this option compared to some of theother ones.

These are just a few of the options that you can go with when it comes to you selling short or buying long. Each trade is going to be a little bit different, so make sure to check each one out and see how they work for your needs. You need to really look into the stock and consider how each one is traded, what may happen according to the patterns that you see, and make sure you can actually earn a profit.

Chapter 10: Planning Limit or Stop Orders

Although allthe patterns we have discussed in this guidebook are great to use, you never want to assume that a pattern is always going to move the way you think. Sometimes, false signals are going to develop and even a pattern that looks strong can go the opposite way you want. When your money is at risk, you also want to make sure that you are able to limit your losses. With the stock market, there is a solution that you can use to make that happen.

To help limit your losses and help plan your own stock strategies, you cantry using stop orders. These are the orders that will work to help limit how much you will lose during the trade and can make your profits bigger. By adding one of these stop orders, you are telling your broker that you want that stop to happen at a certain point in time.

For these though, you are going to involve the market price. Instead of telling your broker to get out in two weeks, you will tell them to get out when the stock reaches a certain price. If the stock never gets to that point, you will stay in the market and make a good profit. But if the stock goes the opposite way you have planned, this helps keep your losses down to a minimum.

Probably, the best reason to consider doing a stop order is that it will make sure you get your emotions out of the game. One problem that a beginner may encounter when they get started with the stock market is that they let their emotions take over. They will get too involved in the trade and make bad decisions in the hopes of earning more profits. For example, they might stay in the market for too long that they end up losing money. Or, they stay in the market even when they start losing money in the hopes of getting it back. When you work with the stop order from the start, you can avoid these emotional issues and actually keep your investment going strong.

Stop Orders

A stop order is going to be done on a trade that is executed up to a specific total. The target price that you want the trade to move is going to become your stop price. Let us say you are working with a stock that can trade at $20. You could have a stop order in place by telling your broker to sell that stock when it reaches $17. The order will be kept in place by your broker.If your stock gets to $1, the trade ends.

This can help you keep the stock where you want it. It can also help youavoid losing so much money. With that stop order, you will get out of the market when it reaches $17. Even if the stock keeps going down to reach $10,you at least got out with a minimal amount of loss. But if you forgot to put that stop order in place, you may be stuck with a bigger loss.

A stop order can come in handy when you want to ensure you will earn a profit as well. You could purchase a stock at

$15 and then, put a stop order in place for $19. When the stock reaches $19, you will sell and make the profit. It is possible that the stock will go back up or go even higher, but there is also a chance that the stock will go lower right away. This helps ensure that you will at least get some profits.

When you look at your graphs, you should be able to see some general trends in the stock you want to work with. You can look at these patterns and determine your stop orders based on that information. That way, you can maximize your profits as much as possible, without having to worry about losing money in the process.

Trailing Stops

Another option you can work with is a trailing stop. This is where you are going to be right behind the market price, but you will make sure that it still has a fixed amount that goes with it. This works well for any stock that is increasing in value. This can also be a very good movetobenefit from the possible gains that come from it. Let us look at an example of a trailing stop and how you would use it when trading.

- You have a stock that has its market value at $30. You may choose to put a trailing stop of $27 on this stock so you have a $3 difference between the stop and the market value.
- When the stock goes up, say to $35, your trailing stop will then move up to $32. In this case, if the stock price goes back down, you will get out at $32 and still make a profit.
- Even if the stock dips down to $33 and then back up to $34, your trailing stop will stay in place. It will only go up and not down,helping you to actually make a profit.
- The stock would go down to $32 after some time. Then, the trailing stop is executed and the trade is complete.

If you did this trade, you would make a profit of $2 on each share. This may not be a huge amount, but it still resulted in a profit and helped you earn money on the trade.

Stop and Reverse

Another option that you can choose is the stop and reverse order. This is a strategy where you take that stop order and place it at a certain point for loss. When this point is reached and the first order is attained and executed, another new order will be placed. This oneis going to be a reverse of what you did on that original order. This can be used if you feel your stock will still go up in value. With this strategy, you will most likely do two separate orders to make it happen.

This is the strategy you would choose to go withif the stock has been identified as the one that willgo up. You may be able to notice an upward pattern to help you forecast that the stock will go up. You can then work with your broker to set a special order to handle this strategy. If the stock does not end up increasing, then, you have taken a big risk on this strategy and you can lose a lot of money. Be careful when you choose this option.

Limit Orders

The limit order will be executed as soon as specific conditions or terms are met. The focus on this is to have the minimum and maximum orders for your trade all in line, and they will only happen when certain conditions are met. While the stop order is going to concentrate more on selling at a specific total, you can have a limit order that talks about multiple values. Here's an example of how you would do a limit order:

1. You would place a limit order on some stock that is trading right now at $15.
2. You would then place a limit order. This is where you would establish a limit of $13. This shows that you are not willing to pay more than $13 to purchase that stock.

3. You can then also set how many shares you are willing to purchase once the stock reaches that $13 mark.
4. At times, you may already own the stock when it is at $15. You can also establish a limit order to help here. You would simply set it to sell the stock at $18. If it suddenly jumps to $20, the limit order would still sell at that point and you would just make more profits.

Now, while these limits and stop orders are really nice and can help protect your investment, they are not a license for you to set up the trade and then forget all about it when the money comes rolling in. They are there to help add some safeguards, but you still need to be an active investor to get the most out of them and to protect your money.

Remember that a computer platform and a brokerage can only go so far when it comes to keeping these limits in check. Sometimes the platformthat you are using is going to miss the signals that stateon how an order should be executed. This is a big problem that could keep an investment from being managed the way you want.

This is especially important when you are working in areally volatile market. Things can change quickly.If the platform does not do your orders at the right times, you could end up losing more money than you planned. Being an active participant, especially if you are doing some short-term trades, can be the best way to protect your money, no matter which strategy you are trying to use.

Chapter 11: How Do I Purchase Stocks on a Margin?

There are times when you want to get in on a good trade, but you find that you do not have the money, or at least enough money, to execute that trade. In some cases, your broker may be willing to allow you to trade on a margin. Buying on a margin is a pretty simple concept. You are going to borrow money from the broker in orderto do the trade that you want. This money can be used to purchase more shares or an expensive stock that you could not do so before.

Buying on the margin can be a really great way to get into more trades, but it can be risky as well. In fact, it is so risky that there aremany brokers who will not allow this kind of strategy unless you have worked with them for a long time, and on many trades, in the past. Let us look at some of the specific rules that come with margin trading so you have a better understanding of how it works.

- To start, you need to work with your broker to get a margin account. This means you usually have to apply for the account. Your margin account is going to be different from your cash account.
- You will need to sign a margin agreement with your broker.The terms of this agreement can include information about how much of a margin you can trade and at what rate.
- You can make a trade if you are approved. An example of this is having $20,000 in the margin account. Then, you see a stock worth $400 a share. You might ask to purchase 100 shares, but that would require you $40,000.
- After you make this trade, the amount of money in your regular accountwill go toward the cost while the rest is a loan from the broker.
- You need to pay back the value of that loan at some point. This often includes interest at the margin rate. If you fail with the trade, you

will still have topay that loan back.
If the stock does well, you can sell
it,pay back the loan, and still take a
profit. It does, however, make
things a bit trickier to accomplish.

- You also need to have your margin
totals in place. Your margin
account could have certain limits
on the amount you are allowed to
borrow at a given time.

The Margin Rate

The margin rate isbasically the interest
your broker is going to charge on the
loan they give you. The broker gets to
determine how much they want to
charge for the margin rate. If they
charged 7 percent on that $20,000 loan,
then, you would have to pay back $1,400
in interest on the margin trade. Some
brokers will charge even more and they
might even depend on how much you
deposited into your account. Make sure
you fully realize the margin rate and how
much it will cost you before getting into
one of these trades. Since you are
borrowing money and starting a loan

with a high interest rate, you do not want to get into something that kind of looks good or might be fun, because it could end up costing you quite a bit.

Strategies to Help with Margin Trading

Margin trading can be a way to make more money. But for the most part, it should only be done after you have a lot of experience with trading in the stock market. The potential for profit grows, but the margin that comes with these trades can make a loss so much worse. If you decide to trade on the margin, there are a few different strategies that you can use to make it more profitable for you. These include:

- *Keep the margins small.* Just because you have the option to trade twice the money does not mean you should do it. The smaller the margin, the less risk you are going to carry on that trade. Consider coming up with most of the money, and then, add a bit of the margin to make the trade stronger.

- *Look for the stop orders.* These stop orders are even more important if you are a margin trader. You can use these stop orders to keep the losses down.
- *Avoid speculation.* Margin trading can make it really easy to become a speculator. But as soon as you do that, you are going to lose a lot of money. Speculation is very problematic because it brings emotions back into the game and can make it hard for you to make smart decisions when trading.
- *High rewards also mean you run into higher risks.* Even though you have the opportunity to trade on the margin and make more money, it still carries a lot of risks. The risk is always greater when you add in more reward to the equation. You are working with more shares and adding more money, along with interest, which makes it really easy to lose much when you do this

option. You need to think carefully about whether trading on the margin is worth the time, effort, and the risk that comes with it.

Trading on the margin can helpincrease your purchasing power. If you see a great trade and are certain that it will yield high profits, this can then be a way for you to jump onto that trade and make a lot of money even if you still have to pay off the loan at the margin rate. But new traders need to be careful when utilizing this option because there are also a lot of risks associated with it. Have a solid strategy and repayment plan in place in case things go wrong, and make sure that you are picking the best stocks for your needs.

Chapter 12: Other Strategies to Help You Make a Profit in the Stock Market

In addition to some of the options we have talked about, there are also a number of other choices you can make when picking out the right strategy for your needs. We are going to look at some of these other strategies that you can consider to get the most out of your investing time.

Day Trading

The first option is day trading. This method of trading is when you purchase a stock and sell it within the same day. Sometimes you will only hold onto the stock for a few minutes or hours. As long as you purchase and sell the stock within the same day, you aredoing day trading. When you do all these small trades, you are able to take advantage of some of the small variations that happen each day with the stock. Even a stable stockor one that is going on an upward trend can have some fluctuations when you look at it each day. A day trader tries to take advantage of this.

The goal of day trading is to purchase the stock when it is below the market average. You will be able to find the market average by looking at charts and other data on a company. You will find that low point and make a purchase. You will keep watching the market and will wait until that stock gets to market value or above. Then, you will trade the stock out and keep the profit.The lower you can purchase the stock and the higher you can sell it in that time period, the more money you can make.

Now, it is unlikely that you will make a lot of money on each individual trade when you are doing day trading. This is because there are only small movements in the market and you will probably not see a big change in either direction in one day. But the point is thatmaking a lot of smaller trades during the day or during the week will add up to a lot of money. When working with day trading though, you must remember that there will be broker fees each time you buy or sell a stock. These fees need to be added in to figure out if you are really making a good profit.

Swing Trading

For some investors, day trading is going to be a little bit restrictive. You have to spend all day watching the market and then, must make the trades very quickly. This is the one that most investors are going to save for when they have some expertise on the market.

Swing trading can come in and solve this problem though. It allows you to have a little more time of usually up to two weeks. You will purchase the stock, often right before a major news announcement is going to be released, and then, sell it within a few weeks after the stock goes back up. This gives you a little more leeway when it comes to how long you hold onto the stock, but it is geared toward helping you make money nowrather than later in the form of dividends.

A swing trader will also concentrate efforts on looking through a technical analysis because they are able to use this information to guess what changes may occur in the near future. They may see that a stock is undervalued, but there is something that is going to raise that stock up in the next few weeks. They will purchase the stock while the prices are low, but when that big event occurs, they will be then able to capitalize on it. The fundamentals are not all that important in this option because you are more concerned about the big changes that will occur in the next few weeks compared to what will happen to the stock over a long time.

Value Investing

Many individuals who get into the stock market like the idea of value investing. The investor who chooses this strategy is looking for any stock that has a lot of strong fundamentals, such as a good amount of dividends, a good book value, earnings, and cash flow. Then, the investor can compare the market price of those stocks to the fundamentals you were calculating. In some cases, the value of the stock is going to be less than what it should be and purchasing the stock at that time means you got ahold of an amazing deal on your investment.

Now, before you choose to go with value investing, you must understand that there is a difference between a junk stock and value investing. Just because a stock is low in price does not mean that it is undervalued and will be able to grow. There are some stocks that keep a low price because they are worthless and are not attached to a good company. These stocks could be worth very little because the company does not have a good debt-to-income ratio or has a bad management.

The value stocks are different. These are the ones that have good earning potential, low debt, and are able to pay dividends to their shareholders. However, there is something that is going on in the market that results to the stock being sold for less than their value.At some point, the market will get better or the people will gain more trust in itand the value will go up for these stocks. This will not happen if you work with junk stocks.

With value investing, you are going to buy the business rather than the stock. They are going to take a look at how the company runs and decide if they want to invest. They will not look at any of the external factors that affect the company, such as a bad economy, but they are instead going to focus on the underlying worth of the company and see if it may go back up at some time.

Technical Analysis

Another option that you can choose to go with is a technical analysis.
Now, there are some people who are not all that fond of using the idea of value

investing. They do not like how it assumes that a stock is underpriced. Instead, they figure that the market price for the stock is what the consumer or the investor is already willing to pay, regardless of the fundamental analysis of that company. Others like this option because it gives them a way to find great deals on a company that they would not be able to invest in without this method.

A technical analyst is going to spend some of their time looking at past trading activity, along with some of the price changes that have occurred with a stock, to see whether the security is strong and how it is going to behave in the future. They are not really going to worry about the value of the company and they do not care at all about whether the company is undervalued. They just look at the charts and figure out where the stock is going in the near future.

If you decide to do a technical analysis of your stock, you need to be able to forecast the way the price is going to move. This can often be determined by the supply and demand of that stock or other security at that time. You will often figure this out by looking at the past prices of the stock, but other times you may want to include figures about volume or interest as well.

Most of the other methods that we have talked about in this guidebook are going to use a technical analysis, including all of those that rely on charts and patterns to help you get the right stock. There are a lot of different technical indicators that you can follow to make it super easy to forecast where a stock price is going. Some will simply look at the current trend of the market. Some will try to see how strong that trend is to determine if it is going to continue in the future.

As a technical analyst, you need to spend time looking at a ton of graphs, not just about the stock you are interested in purchasing, but also for the industry and even the market. This helps you look at the history of the market and better determine how it will go in the future. These patterns are going to give you a good idea of how the security is going to go in the future. You can then make your trades based on that information.

To make your technical analysis work, you need to be good at reading graphs and understanding how the market works. Some of the things that this kind of analysis is going to entail include:

- Gathering graphs and charts about the market and about your chosen stock
- Watching the news to see if there are any predicted changes in the market
- Recognizing trends in the market as well as with your stock to see what may happen in the future
- Making accurate predictions based on this research

A technical analysis is a bit different from the fundamental analysis we talked about earlier. It is meant to look at how the market, as well as the chosen stock, are doing right now price-wise and can make it easier to determine when you should get into trading for the most profits.

All of these strategies can work well to help you when you start investing. The most important part is to learn how to use each one, and then, stick with it when you are in the middle of a trade. If you are able to do all that, you are sure to see some great profits with your investing.

Position Trading

This is another strategy you can choose when you plan to stay in the market for a longer period of time. If you want to do short-term trades, pick day trading or swing trading. Many traders like to go with position trading because it allows them to stay with the same stocks and just keep up with the market, rather than having to switch all the time.

The reason many beginner traders like to go with position trading is because it gives them more time to focus and watch the trends in the market before they make their decisions to either purchase or sell a stock. They are not rushed into the position either way, and they can sometimes wait out the ups and downs of that particular stock.

When you decide to enter into a position trade, you need to take the time to look at your charts. You cannot just enter it and walk away for a few years. You still need to take care of your investment and watch it grow. You will need to watch the weekly and monthly charts because these will help you to make the important decisions that your investment needs.

The good news about the position trading option is that you do not have to worry about the short-term changes that occur in the stock as much as other options do. You can hold onto the position as long as that negative trend reverses itself. You can ride it out, wait until the price goes back up, and then, make a profit on that investment. This takes out some of the worry and stress that can come with investing, which is why many beginners prefer this method.

There are a number of reasons why a trader would want to go with position trading. These can include the following:

- Using the investment to help them in retirement
- Want to earn dividends each quarter as profit
- Less volatility in how much you will make
- You do not need to check the market every day
- You do not have to worry about short-term changes in the market
- The potential to make a lot of money as the company grows

Scalping

Scalping is another option you can work with. It is similar to day trading, but these trades often rely on just a few minutes to make a profit, rather than potentially a whole day.

The idea that comes with scalp trading is that you will make a ton of purchases of a stock and then sell it at a higher price as quickly as possible. You can only hold onto the stock for a day to make a scalp trading, but usually, you will not hold onto that security for more than five or 10 minutes. Sometimes you may be able to purchase a stock when it is on a discount on one of the markets, and then, turn around and sell it higher on a different market just a few minutes later to make a profit.

Any time that you see that there is a momentary down in the market, you are going to purchase the stock. Then, when the stock goes back up to average or above again, you will then sell that same stock. You will keep doing this a lot of these trades throughout the day, earning a small profit on each transaction that will add up to a good amount when you are done.

This works especially well if you see that a stock is selling for really low on one exchange, but there is a higher demand for it on another exchange. You can then purchase when it is low and sell it for a higher amount. You must be careful with this though because there are often fees and other things associated with it and you do not want to lose out on all your profits because of that.

This would also work within the same market though. You may find that there is a stock that seems to have a lot of ups and downs during the day. You can easily purchase the stock when it is at one of its lows so you get it at a good price. You would find these lows by watching the market and learning the trends for that share. Then, when the price goes back up, you would sell the stock again. This process could take just a few minutes to complete, or a few hours depending on the stock and the trendsit follows.

Income Investing

The next option that you can go with is income investing. With this strategy, you want to take a look at companies with the idea that they will provide you with enough money to earn your living, or at least to provide you with a substantial flow of income. It is a simple idea. You just need to look for companies that are paying a high enough dividend that you could live off from that each year.

When you want to find a stock that will provide you with a steady stream of income, you will usually go with a safe option. This option will provide you with some return on investment, but will not have too much risk associated with it. This is why many people go with bonds and income securities, although you can do this with the stock market as well. You just need to find a company that can give you these returns for it to work.

Now, when working with income investing, you must pick a stock that provides its shareholders with a good dividend each quarter, or you will not be able to earn a good income. The average yield for many of the stocks will be three percent. But when you are trying to use this as an income source, you should aim to get six percent or more. This means the company you pick must pay a higher dividend payment than what you will see with others on the stock market or you will not make a good income.

In addition to being able to find a company who has a stock that will produce a steady and a predictable stream of income for you over many years, you should also look at the policies that are in place for the dividends. The income investor should consider whether one of the companies they want to invest inwill continue with the same dividend payment structure going into the future, or are thinking about changing it up.

If you decide to do this one and your research helps you find a company that was able to increase their dividends recently, then, this is something to look in to. You need to ask whether the company will be able to increase these dividends or if they are going to be able to remain steady in the future. If the company was able to do this for the past year straight, then, this is a good company to consider investing your money in.

The best way to ensure that this is going to work is to always do your research and see how a company did in the past. You can also look at some projections for the future as well. These will give you some outlook into whether the company will even pay dividends and if these dividends will be large enough for you to use as income.

Trading in Options

We talked about options a bit earlier.It is important to know how to trade with them if you decide that this is your choice for investing in the stock market. Options are going to be seen as a bit different than what you can do with the stock market. However, they are technically the same thing, so you can definitely do them here.

To keep it simple, an option is basically a derivative of a security. They are this way because the price that you are going to pay for that option is going to be linked to the price of something else. You are gaining a contract that is giving you the right to sell or buy the underlying asset at a predetermined price. You have the option to exercise this right or not though. However, you can only exercise this right either before or on the date that the option expires.

The right for you to purchase that option is known as a call option, and the right to sell that option is known as the put option. If you have heard about futures, you may recognize that there are some similarities here. They are however a bit different. For example, a future is going to make you have the rights and the obligations to purchase the security.With an option, you can choose to let the right pass without doing anything if the market does not work in your favor.

For example, if you would like to purchase some land in the next two years after some city regulations go through, you could purchase an option at $6,000 to provide an incentive for the seller to give it to you. If the regulations go through, the $6,000 will be the deposit towards the investment and you will be able to exercise the right to purchase the land at the price you and the seller agreed to. It does not matter what the market value of the land is at the time the city regulations passes, you will only need to pay what is in the option contract.

If the regulations do not go through and you decide not to purchase the land, you are not obligated to make the purchase. You will lose the $6,000 that you invested, but you do not need to purchase all that land if things do not work out.

This is an example of a commodity that you can purchase with options, but there are also a lot of stocks that you can purchase as options. Make sure to talk this over with your broker to see what stocks are available to do this way through them.

Chapter 13: How to Recognize That a Stock is a Bad Choice

While searching for the right stock in the market, you also need to be aware of some signs that a stock is not a good one to invest in. Some of the problems we are going to look at in this chapter show that a stock is not really doing that well and that itis a difficult investment. Some of the signs you should watch out for when trying to avoid a bad stock include:

The Debt-To-Equity Ratio is High

The first thing you need to check with a stock is whether the debt-to-equity ratio of the underlying business has started to increase. There are times when a business will start to rack up some extra debt. The reason it does this is the important part. If they gain more debt because they are acquiring a new patent or expanding, then it is not such a big deal. But if they have this debt because of an underperforming asset, a lawsuit, or excessive loans, it is a bad thing and you need to avoid this as much as possible.

Any business that has a high debt-to-equity ratio may not last long. They do not have enough leverage to work with so it is hard for the stock to maintain itself or manage. You should pick another stock to work with instead.

The Company's Cash Flow is Negative

There is always the chance that the stock you are looking at has a negative cash flow. When this happens, the cash flow that goes outward is going to be greater than the cash the business is earning. Sometimes, this could be because the business is using a lot of its money to expand. In some other cases, it shows that the company is unable to manage its assets in the proper manner.

Regardless of the reason, it is important to take this negative cash flow as a big warning sign that the stock may not be the best one to invest in. The best strategy is to inspect the stock to find out why the business has a negative cash flow to start with. This could be a sign of the business growing and they are just spending that money to thrive. If this is true, then, you can still consider that stock for purchase. But it could also be a big sign that the business is collapsing and you need to watch out for that.

Profit Warnings

As you are working with some of the news reading strategies, make sure that you learn to watch out for some of the profit warnings. This type of warning is a difficult report that is going to show how a company may not be doing as well as it had hoped. A company will release a report that basically says they are not going to meet their expectations, although they often hide it in other wordings and flowery prose. Make sure to keep a close eye on all your news readings to figure if there might be a price warning that you need to be aware of.

Insider Trading is Very Prominent

Insider trading is a serious problem, and it is also illegal. It is going to occur when people trade on a stock because they get insider information, which is supposed to be confidential. This illegal advantage can make the value of a stock change very quickly.

A company is supposed to report if some of its shares are bought by an insider, such as high-value shareholders or company directors. It has to explain who these insiders are, why they are investing in the stock, and how many shares they are going to buy. This ensures that people will have an idea why a stock is moving to a certain value. Insider trading can be a problem because those inside the company could pull off some trades to help make the value of a stockwork in their favor without worrying about spending time on producing a report.

A High-LevelResignation Happens in the Company

The next issue that can tell you whether a stock is a bad one to go with is if there is a high-level resignation. When someone decides to resign from a position, there is a period of uncertainty in the market. If anything, it will show that a serious change could happen with that stock. This becomes a bigger problem if the person who resigns is not open about it. This could cause the value of the stock to go down.

Now, when someone resigns, it can have a negative impact on the stock. But if someone retires off the board, it is not going to really affect the stock. You should still watch it just in case, but the odds of the stock plummeting in value is not very likely. It often depends on how prominent that person was and how much influence they had over the whole company.

An Investigation by the SEC

An SEC investigation can occur at any time the business is believed to be doing something wrong. This can sometimes give off the impression that the stock is not doing any good because the business does not appear to be as strong as people think. A stock could be hurt by this type of investigation. These investigations are serious and you need to take precautions if you already own the stock because the value may be heading down.

Other Common Things to Watch with a Bad Stock

The following signs are ones that the stock is in trouble and you should not go with it. These are basic signs that might not show how a stock is going to lose money, but they may mean that the stock is going to have a harder time producing a profit for you. Some of the signs that you should watch out for include:

- A stock might be trading just above $10 a share for a long time, but it recently decreased to $10 or below.
- A stock ends up going through a big price decrease of 15 percent to 25 percent of its value in a short amount of time. You should definitely do some research to find out why this big drop happened.
- The value of the stock seems to reach a plateau and is not keeping up with the market at all.
- The earnings that come out for that stock are declining in value. Earnings consistently dropping every year can be a big problem for the company and for the investor. It is one thing to see the earnings decrease for a year, but it can be very concerning when this happens more often.
- The total volume of debt that is inside a particular company starts growing.

- The sales numbers and other financial factors end up looking small and meaningless when you compare them to how the competitor is doing.
- The P/E ratio is a lot higher than you would like to see in businesses of that same industry. It is even more concerning when you are not able to find a reason for why this ratio is going up in value rather than meeting the average for that industry.

With all of these signs that show how a stock is declining, you may have the assumption that you can just do a put order. In some cases, this willwork.But in others, it is more about the stocks being in serious trouble, and a put order will not be able to save you. You have to be careful about investing in stocks with these signals because they can often guarantee that you are going to lose money on that trade.

Now, there is always a chance for a stock to rebound after just a few days, or even after a few weeks. The rebound sometimes occurs simply because the stock finally gets cheap enough that it shows as a discount and some people are excited to get in on it. This does not always happen so you need to always do your research and due diligence before you decide to trade or invest in a stock.

Chapter 14: Easy Tips to Help You Make the Most Money on the Stock Market

When you first get started in the stock market, there are a lot of things that you need to figure out. You have to come up with a savings amount so you can spend. You have to pick out a good platform to actually earn you money. And you need a solid stock and a good strategy to ensure that you can actually make money out of all this. This chapter is going to help make it easier for you by exploring some things you can do to get the most out of your stock market investment.

Find a Strategy That Works for You

As this guidebook went over, there are a lot of different strategies you can choose to try out to make money in the stock market. Some are really easy to use, while some are a bit more difficult. Some are going to work in a bullish market and others work better in a bearish market. There is a strategy that works well for everyone. You just need to find the right one for you.

Working in the stock market brings a lot of challenges, but one way to reduce these is by choosing a strategy and sticking with it. Too many investors start out with a strategy but find that it is not working for them or the market is turning in a different way than planned. They panic and quickly try to make some changes to save their investment.

Changing strategies right in the middle of a trade is a bad idea. It just would not work because each of them relies on different patterns to get the work done. If you start a trade and find that you are not that fond of it, it is fine for you to try out a new one. Just make sure that the particular trade has concluded before you move on to the new strategy.

As a beginner, you may try out a few different types of strategies to find the one that works best for you. But the important thing is to research them well and really know what you are looking

into when you first getstarted. This
ensures that you are able to give the
strategy your full attention and effort
before you move on.

Set Those Stop Points

We spent some time in this guidebook
talking about the stop points and limit
points to keep your losses down to a
minimum. Some new investors figure
they can watch the market on their own,
and they do not take the time to actually
work on these stop points and try to save
themselves. These stop points are there
to protect you in case you made a wrong
prediction or in case the market goes
completely wrong.

You can set a stopping point that is
regular or trailing, or you can choose to
go with an option for losing and for
making profits. This ensures you earn as
much as possible and limits your risks.
You still need to spend some time
researching and watching the market to
ensure that the stock is performing the

way that you want. But these stop points can certainly make it easier for a beginner and can save them some risk.

Leave Emotions out of the Game

Emotions are going to be your worst nightmare when you get started on the stock market. As soon as you let those emotions out, you will start to make some bad trades that will harm your ability to make money on the stock market. Once those emotions are setin place, your investment is going to be at risk. You will make poor decisions and leave your strategy in the dust.

For those who tend to give in to their emotions, it is best for you to find another form of investing. The stock market can be great, but it does have a lot of fluctuations and it is possible that you could lose all of your money if you are not careful.

Your emotions can lead you to stay in the stock market for too long. Sometimes we think that a trade will keep going up and we should stick with it to make enormous profits. But the market does level out over time and if you stay in too long, you may see the market turn on you and you will lose money.

It can go against you the other way too. If you see that you are losing money, then, get out and preserve your investment. Many new investors will stay in the market, even when they are losing, because they think they can get that money back if they just stay in for a little longer.

In either of these situations, you would have seen that the trend was going to reverse. The charts we have been talking about this whole guidebook can help you notice when a trend is about to occur, and you can make the appropriate changes and work to get in and out of the trades at the right time. Sometimes this will save you from losing too much money in the process, and other times it will help you earn money.

Try out Some Platforms Before Deciding

You should take some time trying out a few platforms before you decide which one is the best for your needs. Some platforms are just easier to work with, while some may have lag times that could make you lose money. Some will just have more features than others. Each trader is going to find that different aspects are important to them, and knowing which aspects are the most important for you can help you pick out a platform.

Often, youget a trial run on these platforms before you decide to use them. If you get this option, take your time. You want to explore the platform. Maybe do a practice run with a trade, and be very thorough. You are going to use this platform to help you make money in the stock market. Because of this, you want to make sure that the platform works properly and has everything you need to make trading aseasy as possible.

Learn the fees That Each Broker Charges

Each broker is going to charge a different fee for working with them. Some are going to focus their fees on each individual trade. Others are going to charge a commission from what you earn. The one that you go with can sometimes depend on the type of trading you want to work with.

For example, if you plan to do just a few long-term trades and enjoy earning dividends on those companies for a long time to come, then, going with a flat rate per trade is probably going to be the best. If you are not trading that much, then, these flat fees are not going to cut into your profits that much.

If you choose to go with something like day trading, you may want to lean more toward the commissions. The commission ensures that you only pay a little bit out of pocket, rather than having to pay each time you do a trade. Day trading can involve a lot of little trades over the course of the day. Each trade may only net you a little bit of money, but if you are able to do that a bunch of times, you will earn a higher profit. But if you are paying $5 per trade, you will have a hard time keeping up with day trading.

Find a Mentor

The next thing that you can try to do is to find a mentor to work with. There are many people who have spent time in the stock market and have learned the right tips and tricks to make the most out of their money with the fewest dollars out of their pocket. If you can find someone who is willing to work with you and show you the ropes, you are going to be way ahead of everyone else whojust got started in the stock market.

This does not mean that you should just blindly follow what your mentor tells you. With the stock market, you need to follow your own gut and intuition and listen to the risks that you are willing to take and nothing else. Your mentor is sure to give you a lot of advice. Some of the advice will be good, but you need to pay attention to what you feel comfortable doing and make some of your own decisions. The money you spend in the stock market is yours, so treat it as such and you will make some great trades.

Try Working with Dogs of the Dow While You Get Used to the Market

One easy strategy to use when you first start in the stock market is the Dogs of the Dow. Each year, a new list of the best-performing stocks on the market is released. You would simply look at this list and invest in the top 10. This allows you to have time to diversify your portfolio quite a bit.Most stocks on this list are doing well and are secure, so you get the added bonus of having dividend payments without having to lookhard at charts and figure.

When the year ends, you go through and checkthe list again. There are times when you may have to change the stocks you are trading because they are no longer in the top 10 of this list. It is an easy way for a beginner to diversify their portfolio, make some money, and get some time to learn about the market before jumping in.

This does not mean that you can just purchase the stocks and not look at them for a year. This strategy is a great one for beginners because it is often better than what other strategies have. There are still times when a stock on this list will fall or run into trouble. Even if you go with this option, make sure to take it slowly and watch the stocks to make sure you keep earning money on your investments.

If You Do a Bad Trade, Consider Taking a Break

There are times when one of your trades is going to be less than stellar. You may have read the charts the wrong way, jumped into a trade too quickly, or just made overall bad trading decisions in the hopes of making a lot of money quickly. If you go through a particularly bad trade, it may be best for you to take a few days off from trading.

Many new traders run into problems when they have a bad trade and do not take off a few days. They get emotionally involved. They feel bad about losing that money, and they want to be able to earn it back as quickly as possible. They often get caught up in revenge trading, where they will try to take bigger and bigger risks in the hopes of earning that money back. But since they are only focused on making money back quickly, they are going to make really bad decisions that will cause them to lose even more money.

The break does not have to be a long one. A week is plenty of time for most people. It, however, gives you the chance to take a step back, look at your trading strategy, and see if you need to make changeswithout emotions associated with the loss getting in the way.

Getting started on the stock market can be a great experience. You have the potential to make a lot of money in a short amount of time, or even over the long-term, as long as you make good and sound decisions. Follow some of the tips in this chapter, and you will be trading in the stock market like a professional in no time.

Conclusion

Thank for making it through to the end of *Stock Market Investing for Beginners*.Let us hope it was informative and was able to provide you with all the tools you need to achieve your goals.

The next step is to decide how you want to get into the market. There are a lot of choices when it comes to how you would like to invest your money, but the stock market offers the most diversity out of all of them. You can choose which company you want to invest in, how long you want to stay in the market, and how much you want to invest.

This guidebook took some time to look over all the options that you have when it comes to investing in the stock market. We looked at the basics of the stock market, some of the different types of securities that you can choose, and the best strategies that will help you make a profit each time you do a trade. We even spent time talking about trading the margin, how to know when a stock is a good one or not, and the best tips to get the most out of trading even when you are just starting.

When you are ready to get started with your investment in the stock market, make sure to check this guidebook to help youmake a profit and put your money to work for you.

Finally, if you found this book useful in anyway, a review on Amazon is always appreciated!

www.ingramcontent.com/pod-product-compliance
Lightning Source LLC
Chambersburg PA
CBHW071418210326
41597CB00020B/3558